OOOKY POOKY SPOOKY FEAR

TELLING FEAR TO GO AWAY!

WRITTEN BY DIAN LAYTON Song Stories ILLUSTRATED BY JD HORNBACHER

DESTINY IMAGE® PUBLISHERS, INC.
P.O. Box 310, Shippensburg, PA 17257-0310
"Promoting Inspired Lives."

Illustrations by JD Hornbacher

This book and all other Destiny Image and Destiny Image Fiction books are available at Christian bookstores and distributors worldwide.

For more information on foreign distributors, call 717-532-3040.
Or reach us on the Internet: www.destinyimage.com

ISBN 13 TP: 978-0-7684-4991-4
ISBN 13 eBook: 978-0-7684-4992-1
ISBN 13 HC: 978-0-7684-5021-7

For Worldwide Distribution, Printed in the U.S.A.

1 2 3 4 5 6 7 8 9 10 11 / 23 22 21 20 19 18

OOOKY POOKY SPOOKY FEAR

TELLING FEAR TO GO AWAY!

WRITTEN BY
DIAN LAYTON

ILLUSTRATED BY
JD HORNBACHER

INTRODUCTION

FEAR.

It's a huge issue in the lives of children (and adults as well).

Instead of saying "don't be afraid," let's help kids know what to DO when they ARE afraid.

The visual image we've chosen to portray fear is a dragon; a rude, nasty and very disgusting dragon. You might be familiar with the "SEEKER" books - an allegorical series where kids learn to overcome dragons like Anger, Discouragement and Fear. The Oooky Pooky Spooky Fear song is from the first Seeker story, when Seeker learns to command the dragon fear to GO AWAY - in the King's Name!

In this "song-story", the dragon seems to be huge and overwhelming, but when the characters face their fears and tell the dragon to GO AWAY in the Name of the King - then fear loses its power. The illustrations show the dragon actually trembling with fear because of the children's confidence!

This book deals with three main fears that kids face: fear of the dark, fear of abandonment and fear OF and WITHIN bullies. (One main reason that people bully other people is that they themselves are driven by fear.)

It is our sincere prayer that this "song-story" will be an effective tool to help children overcome and conquer their fears.

On with the Adventure!

DIAN & JD

WELL YOU JUST GOTTA STOP, STOP AND THINK
AND REMEMBER WHAT TO DO.
EVERY FEAR WILL DISAPPEAR – WHEN YOU SING!
AND HERE'S THE SONG I USE...

That's the song to sing,
So sing it loud;
That's the song to sing,
So sing it now!

Oooky pooky spooky fear,
You have no right to come near…

Oooky pooky spooky fear,
You have no right to come near!

In the King's Name you get outta here,
Fear be gone, be gone; Fear be gone!

What are YOU afraid of?

Did you know there is a very real King, whose Name
is SO powerful it can make fear run and hide?
That King is **Jesus**.
He tells us that we don't have to be afraid, because He
has already rescued the world from the power of fear.
And he WANTS you to call on His name and make fear
GO AWAY!
Because when fear has no power over you, then our great
King can use **you** to help **others** get free. And King Jesus'
Story - His big, true Story - is the best story of all.

DIAN & JD

TALK ABOUT IT TIME

What parts of this "song-story" did you enjoy?

What happened to the dragon of fear each time
the children stood up to it?

The next time you feel afraid, what will you do?

What advice would you give to someone who is afraid?

Read these verses from the King's Great Book, the Bible:
Psalm 8:2, Isaiah 41:10-13, 2 Timothy 1:7

At **www.dianlayton.com** you can get the
"Oooky Pooky Spooky Fear" SONG, the SEEKER books,
and other great materials!
AND at that website - you can find out how to get a caricature
(picture) by the artist, JD Hornbacher, of **YOU** conquering fear!

ABOUT THE AUTHOR

Dian Layton lives in Alberta, Canada. She loves taking kids and families on storytelling adventures; and one of her favorite adventures is to help kids get rid of fear! Check out her books, music and curriculum at www.dianlayton.com.

ABOUT THE ARTIST

JD Hornbacher lives in Alberta, Canada with his wife and three kids. He is a Children's Pastor and a Media Producer, and he is obsessed with Jesus, church, family, and comic books.